The Leap

I0141065

Gavin Kostick

methuen | drama

LONDON • NEW YORK • OXFORD • NEW DELHI • SYDNEY

METHUEN DRAMA

Bloomsbury Publishing Plc, 50 Bedford Square, London, WC1B 3DP, UK
Bloomsbury Publishing Inc, 1359 Broadway, New York, NY 10018, USA
Bloomsbury Publishing Ireland, 29 Earlsfort Terrace, Dublin 2,
D02 AY28, Ireland

BLOOMSBURY, METHUEN DRAMA and the Methuen
Drama logo are trademarks of Bloomsbury Publishing Plc.

First published in Great Britain 2025

Cover illustration by Steve McCarthy

Cover concept by Publicis Dublin

A catalogue record for this book is available from the British Library.

A catalog record for this book is available from the Library of Congress.

ISBN: PB: 978-1-3505-9627-6
ePDF: 978-1-3505-9628-3
eBook: 978-1-3505-9629-0

Series: Plays for Young People

Typeset by Mark Heslington Ltd, Scarborough, North Yorkshire

For product safety related questions contact
productsafety@bloomsbury.com.

To find out more about our authors and books visit
www.bloomsbury.com and sign up for our newsletters.

ABOUT FISHAMBLE

Fishamble is an Irish theatre company that discovers, develops and produces new plays of national importance with a global reach. It has toured its productions to audiences throughout Ireland and to twenty-one other countries. It champions the role of the playwright, typically supporting over 50 per cent of the writers of all new plays produced on the island of Ireland each year. Fishamble has received many awards in Ireland and internationally, including an Olivier Award.

'excellent Fishamble . . . Ireland's terrific Fishamble'
The Guardian

'Ireland's leading new writing company' **The Stage**

'the much-loved Fishamble [is] a global brand with international theatrical presence . . . an unswerving force for new writing' **The Irish Times**

'the respected Dublin company . . . forward-thinking Fishamble' **The New York Times**

'when Fishamble is [in New York], you've got to go'
Time Out New York

'that great Irish new writing company, Fishamble'
Lyn Gardner, Stage Door

'the superb Irish company Fishamble'
The Scotsman

'Fishamble puts electricity into the National grid of dreams'
Sebastian Barry

Fishamble Staff: Jim Culleton (Artistic Director and CEO), Eva Scanlan (Executive Director), Gavin Kostick (Literary Manager), Laura MacNaughton (Producer), Sarah Bragg-Bolger (General Manager), Allie Whelan (Marketing, Outreach and Engagement Manager), Evie McGuinness (Assistant Producer), Eimear Hussey (Literary Assistant)

Fishamble is funded by the Arts Council, Dublin City Council, and Culture Ireland.

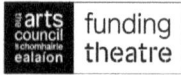

arts council / funding theatre — Comhairle Cathrach Bhaile Átha Cliath / Dublin City Council — Cultúr Éireann / Culture Ireland — Promoting Irish Arts Worldwide for 20 years

First time and early career playwrights

Fishamble has produced many plays by first time playwrights, including *Don Juan* by Michael West in 1990, *Howling Moons, Silent Sons* by Deirdre Hines in 1991, *The Ash Fire* by Gavin Kostick in 1992, *Red Roses and Petrol* by Joseph O'Connor in 1994, *From Both Hips* by Mark O'Rowe in 1997, *The Nun's Wood* by Pat Kinevane in 1998 and *Noah and the Tower Flower* by Sean McLoughlin (Irish Times Best New Play Award winner) in 2007. Many of these plays won the Stewart Parker Trust Award for new playwrights. Recent plays by new and emerging writers include:

- *The Black Wolfe Tone* by Kwaku Fortune (2025), touring in Ireland and New York, in co-production with the Irish Repertory Theatre
- *In Two Minds* by Joanne Ryan (2023–25) touring in Ireland, UK and US
- *Breaking* by Amy Kidd (2024) in Dublin Theatre Festival and on tour
- *Duck Duck Goose* by Caitríona Daly (2021–22) touring in Ireland and online
- *The Humours of Bandon* by Margaret Mc Auliffe (since 2017) touring in Ireland, UK, US and Australia
- *Charolais* by Noni Stapleton (2017) in New York
- *Swing* by Steve Blount, Peter Daly, Gavin Kostick and Janet Moran (2014–16) touring in Ireland, UK, Europe, US, Australia and New Zealand
- *The Wheelchair on My Face* by Sonya Kelly (2013–14) touring in Ireland, UK, Europe and US, winner of Scotsman Fringe First Award.

Established playwrights

Fishamble has ongoing relationships with many of Ireland's top playwrights. Recent productions include:

- *Heaven* by Eugene O'Brien (2022–25) touring in Ireland, UK and US, winner of Scotsman Fringe First, Irish

Times Best Play and Irish Times Best Actress (for Janet Moran) awards

- *Mustard* by Eva O'Connor (2020–24) on tour in Ireland, internationally and online, in co-production with Sunday's Child, winner of Scotsman Fringe First Award
- *The Pride of Parnell Street* by Sebastian Barry (2007–11, and 2022) touring in Ireland and internationally, BBC Audio, multi award-winning
- *On Blueberry Hill* by Sebastian Barry (2017–21) touring in Ireland, Europe, Off-Broadway, West End, Audible and online
- *Rathmines Road* by Deirdre Kinahan (2018) in co-production with the Abbey Theatre
- *Mainstream* by Rosaleen McDonagh (2016) in co-production with Project Arts Centre
- *Little Thing, Big Thing* by Donal O'Kelly (2014–16) touring in Ireland, UK, Europe, US and Australia, winner of The Stage Award
- *Spinning* by Deirdre Kinahan (2014) at Dublin Theatre Festival.

Pat Kinevane

Fishamble is very proud of its long-term relationship with Pat Kinevane whose solo plays it has commissioned, developed, produced and toured since 2006. These are *Forgotten* (since 2006), *Silent* (since 2011), *Underneath* (since 2014), *Before* (since 2018) and *King* (since 2023). These productions have toured in Ireland, UK, Europe, US, Australia, New Zealand and online, in English, and bilingually in many countries. Fishamble and Pat Kinevane have won Olivier, Herald Angel, Stage Raw, Scotsman Fringe First, Herald Archangel, Argus Angel, Origin Best Production and Helen Hayes awards.

International play development partnerships

Fishamble often partners with other arts organisations to develop new work, often by artists who have been underrepresented in Irish theatre. For instance, *Turning Point* in 2010 was a festival of work by Irish writers with disabilities in partnership with ADI and VSA, which toured to the Kennedy Center in Washington DC. Recent initiatives include:

- *Not Beckett* by Jennifer Barclay, Felispeaks, Olwen Fouéré, Hannah Khalil and Nicola McCartney (2024–25), in partnership with the Irish Repertory Theatre, Villanova, Reading University, Citizens Theatre
- *Transatlantic Commissions Residency* by Felispeaks, Kwaku Fortune, Jade Jordan and CN Smith (2024) in Dublin and New York, in partnership with the Irish Repertory Theatre
- *Murdered Men Do Drip and Bleed* by Hannah Khalil and Jennifer Barclay (2023), in Dublin and online, in partnership with Washington DC companies Mosaic and Solas Nua
- *On the Horizon* by Shannon Yee, Hefin Robinson, Michael Patrick, Oisín Kearney, Samantha O'Rourke, Ciara Elizabeth Smyth, Connor Allen (2021) online, in association with Dirty Protest.

Political plays

Fishamble has produced many plays that help us grapple with the world in which we live, sometimes focusing on historical events as part of the government's Decade of Centenaries programme. Many of these productions are site-specific or happen off-site. These include:

- *'Certain Individual Women'* by Julie Morrissy (2024) on national tour
- *Outrage* by Deirdre Kinahan (2022 and 2024) touring and online, in association with Dublin Port Company and Meath County Council
- *The Treaty* by Colin Murphy (2021–22) in Ireland, Irish Embassy in London and online as part of the Seóda Festival

- *Embargo* by Deirdre Kinahan (2020) online, during Dublin Theatre Festival, in association with Dublin Port Company and Irish Rail
- *The Alternative* by Oisín Kearney and Michael Patrick (2019) in association with Pavilion Theatre, Draíocht, Belltable, Everyman Theatre, Town Hall Theatre and Lyric Theatre, winner of Irish Times Best Sound Design (for Denis Clohessy) and Best Director (for Jim Culleton) awards
- *Haughey|Gregory* by Colin Murphy (2018–19) in the Abbey Theatre, Mountjoy Prison, Dáil Éireann, Croke Park and Larkin Community College, as well as on national tour
- *Maz & Bricks* by Eva O'Connor (2017–18) in Ireland, UK and US
- *GPO 1818* by Colin Murphy (2018) staged in the GPO to mark its bicentenary
- *Inside the GPO* by Colin Murphy (2016) performed in the GPO on the centenary of the Easter Rising and screened internationally online
- *Tiny Plays for Ireland and America* by twenty-six writers (2016) at the Kennedy Center, Washington DC, and Irish Arts Center, New York, as part of *Ireland 100*
- *Bailed Out* (2015) and *Guaranteed* (2013) by Colin Murphy, on national tour.

International touring

Many of Fishamble's productions have toured internationally, in partnership with a network of festival and venue partners, including: Soho Theatre, Trafalgar Theatre, Southwark Playhouse, Kiln, Arcola in London; Traverse, Summerhall, Assembly in Edinburgh; 59E59 Theaters, Origin, Irish Arts Center, Irish Repertory Theatre in New York; Odyssey in LA; APA, Merrigong, Vessel in Australia. Recent international tours include:

- *Forgotten, Silent, Underneath, Before,* and *King* by Pat Kinevane (ongoing), to twenty countries

- *The Black Wolfe Tone* by Kwaku Fortune (2025), touring in Ireland and New York, in co-production with the Irish Repertory Theatre
- *In Two Minds* by Joanne Ryan (2023–25) touring in Ireland, UK and US
- *Heaven* by Eugene O'Brien (2022–25) touring in Ireland, UK and US
- *Fight Night* by Gavin Kostick (2025) in New York, in association with Rise Productions
- *Taigh/Tŷ/Teach* by Eva O'Connor, Màiri Morrison, and Mared Llywelyn Williams (2024–25) in Kerry, touring to Scotland and Wales, online and in cinemas, in partnership with Theatre Gu Leòr and Theatr Bara Caws
- *On Blueberry Hill* by Sebastian Barry (2017–21) touring in Ireland, Europe, Off-Broadway, West End, Audible and online
- *Mustard* by Eva O'Connor (since 2020) on tour in Ireland, internationally and online
- *The Humours of Bandon* by Margaret McAuliffe (since 2017) touring in Ireland, UK, US and Australia
- *Drip Feed* by Karen Cogan (2018) in coproduction with Soho Theatre, touring in Ireland and UK
- *Little Thing, Big Thing* by Donal O'Kelly (2014–16) touring in Ireland, UK, Europe, US and Australia
- *Swing* by Steve Blount, Peter Daly, Gavin Kostick and Janet Moran (2014–16) touring in Ireland, UK, Europe, US, Australia and New Zealand.

Other artforms and media

Fishamble often shares filmed versions of its plays online, in cinemas, and through its Encore programme in schools. It produced a series of radio plays for RTÉ lyric fm, and has also recorded audio versions of its productions for Audible, BBC and RTÉ Radio One. It has worked across disciplines, including *Invitation to a Journey* by David Bolger, Deirdre Gribbin and Gavin Kostick (2016) in co-production with

CoisCeim, Crash Ensemble and Galway International Arts Festival. It produced two seasons of tiny plays online:

- *Tiny Plays for a Brighter Future* by Niall Murphy, Signe Lury, Eva-Jane Gaffney (2021) online, in association with ESB
- *Tiny Plays 24/7* by Lora Hartin, Maria Popovic, Ciara Elizabeth Smyth, Caitríona Daly, Conor Hanratty, Julia Marks, Patrick O'Laoghaire, Eric O'Brien, Grace Lobo, Ryan Murphy (2020) online.

Fishamble wishes to thank the following Friends of Fishamble and Corporate Members for their invaluable support:

Alan Ashe, ATM Accounting Services, Dearbhail and Michael Bermingham, Doireann Ní Bhriain, Colette and Barry Breen, John Butler, Betsy Carroll, Breda Cashe, Maura Connolly, Jackie Cronin, Finola Earley, John and Yvonne Healy, Nancy E. Jones, Geoffrey and Jane Keating, Stephen and Susan Lambert, Damian Lane, Angus Laverty, Patrick Lonergan, Sheelagh Malin, Monica McInerney, Patrick McIntyre, Ger McNaughton, Anne McQuillan, Mary Monks Hatch, Liz Morrin, Pat Moylan, Ronan Nulty, Lisney, PwC, Tom O'Connor, Siobhan O'Leary, Andrew and Delyth Parkes, Judy Regan, Royal County Furniture, Jennifer Russell, Eileen Ryan, Colleen Savage, Catherine Santoro, Brian Singleton, William Smith, Eddie Soye and Mary Stephenson.

fishamble.com   facebook.com/fishamble
twitter.com/fishamble

Acknowledgements

Thanks to the following for their help with this production: Maureen Kennelly, Liz Meaney, Bea Kelleher, Maeve Giles, Ciara Coyne, Jesse Weaver, and all at the Arts Council; Ray Yeates, Sinéad Connolly, and all at Dublin City Council Arts Office; all at 3 Great Denmark Street; Máire O'Higgins and all at Larkin Community College; Róise Goan and all at Dublin Theatre Festival, Emer McGowan, Nicola Murphy, John McCabe, Emma Áine O'Leary and all at Draíocht; Olivia Brody, Fiona O'Neill, Shaday Bates and all at NEIC; Aideen Howard, Clodagh Mooney Duggan and all at the Ark; Wayne Jordan; Michael Glenn Murphy; Danielle Galligan; all those who have helped since this publication went to print.

Fishamble: The New Play Company presents

The Leap

By Gavin Kostick

Cast

Wendy	Penny Morris
Dad	Emmet Kirwan

With Shauna Harris and Mary-Lou McCarthy

Creative Team

Playwright	Gavin Kostick
Director	Veronica Coburn
Set and Costume Design	Deirdre Dwyer
Lighting Design	Suzie Cummins
Music and Sound Design	Denis Clohessy
Puppet Design and Fabrication	Ger and Maeve Clancy
Assistant Director	Chloe Naomi (Lir Academy placement)
Artistic Director	Jim Culleton

Production Team

Producer	Laura MacNaughton
Assistant Producer	Evie Mc Guinness
Production Manager	Eoin Kilkenny
Stage Manager	Steph Ryan
Chief LX	Archer Bradshaw
Deputy Production Manager	Laura Murphy
Sound Assistant	John Norton
Costume Asssitant	Toni Bailey
Irish Translation	Emma Finegan
Set Construction	ArtFX.ie
Marketing	Allie Whelan
PR	O'Doherty Communications
General Manager	Sarah Bragg-Bolger
Executive Director	Eva Scanlan

The production runs for approximately 60 minutes, with no interval.

The Leap was developed with the support of the Children's Council at the Ark, facilitated by Shaun Dunne. The production previewed in Larkin Community College, Marino College and Mount Carmel Secondary School, and opened in Draíocht as part of the Dublin Theatre Festival in October 2025. It was made possible by support from Dublin City Council's North East Inner City Initiative.

Biographies

Gavin Kostick is a playwright, literary manager and independent dramaturg.

His works have been produced nationally and internationally. Favourite works for Fishamble include *The Ash Fire, The Flesh Addict, The End of the Road* and *Invitation to a Journey* (with CoisCéim and Crash Ensemble). *The Leap* is Gavin's first play for children.

Further works include *This is What We Sang* for Kabosh, *Fight Night, The Games People Play* and *At the Ford* for Rise Productions and *Gym Swim Party* with Danielle Galligan in co-production with the O'Reilly Theatre. He wrote the libretto for the opera *The Alma Fetish* composed by Raymond Deane, performed at the National Concert Hall. As a performer he performed Joseph Conrad's *Heart of Darkness: Complete*, a six hour show for Absolut Fringe, Dublin Theatre Festival and the London Festival of Literature at the Southbank.

Gavin is currently the literary manager of Fishamble: The New Play Company, a tutor in playwriting and dramaturgy in both The Lir Academy and Trinity College Dublin as well as being a core mentor on the Tenderfoot Transition Year programme for young writers at the Civic Theatre.

Particular favourite projects that Gavin has initiated and delivered with Fishamble include Show in a Bag (with Dublin Fringe and the Irish Theatre Institute), the New Play Clinic, the Dublin Fringe New Writing Award, Tiny Plays for Ireland and A Play for Ireland.

Both for Fishamble, and as an independent dramaturg, Gavin's projects and works he has supported have gained significant national and international award recognition including amongst others the Irish Times Irish Theatre Awards, BBC Stewart Parker Trust, Zebbie Awards, Dublin Fringe Awards, Business to Arts, Olivier, Scotsman Fringe

First, Herald Angel and Archangel and New York Critics' Pick.

His own plays have also received similar national and international award recognition. Gavin has recently completed a new version of *The Odyssey*, supported by Kilkenny Arts Festival, ClassicsNow.

Veronica Coburn is a theatre artist of some forty years' experience.

She has acted as artistic director on a number of ambitious, large scale visionary projects. Draíocht Arts Centre's Home Theatre (Ireland) in 2018 which saw thirty professional playwrights paired with thirty people, Hosts, who lived in Dublin 15. Each playwright wrote an original piece, twenty minutes long, inspired by their Host. All thirty original plays were performed in the Hosts' homes, their kitchens, their living rooms, mapping the stories of the people of D15. And Nest, Draíocht's follow up project to Home Theatre (Ireland). All Nest hosts were children and young people, the youngest Host was twenty days old and the oldest Host was twenty-three years old. Nest culminated in a festival, Spréacha Soar, in March 2024 to celebrate the lives and worlds of our youngest citizens.

Veronica has completed a number of big participatory projects in the Civic Theatre. *Songs of Change*, a response to life under lockdown, culminated in ten original songs inspired by the lived experience of people in South Dublin County and *Ghost Hares*, an SDCC Public Art Commission, celebrating the people and landscape of South Dublin County using spoken and sung text and original song.

She served as artistic director of the National Youth Theatre from 2018–21 with the task of articulating an artistic vision for the programme. In that capacity she directed both Carys D. Coburn's *Ask Too Much Of Me* and Ciara Elizabeth Smyth's *Aftertaste*. She also established ARTiculate, Youth Theatre

Ireland's young playwright programme designed to support and empower young playwrights and theatre makers. ARTiculate was facilitated by Carys D. Coburn and culminated in the production of *Like We Were Born To Move* by ARTiculate graduate, Eimear Hussey, for NYT 2023.

Veronica has been programme director of Tenderfoot, the Civic Theatre's apprentice theatre programme for transition year students since its inception in 2007. A volume of Tenderfoot plays, plays written by and for young people, was published 2015. A book documenting the work of Tenderfoot, *The Mess*, will be published in 2027. Veronica is a Civic Theatre Associate Artist since 2017.

Veronica's directorial work includes *Absent The Wrong*, Carys D. Coburn's play about adoption and family in Ireland (Best Production DFF 2022), *Bernarda's House*, her own red nose version of Lorca's *House of Bernarda Alba*, Amy Conroy's *Eternal Rising of the Sun* and *Break*, Ruth Lehane's *The Lehane Trilogy* and Wicked Angels' *I'm Not A.D.H.D. I'm B.O.L.D.* She also directed Carys D. Coburn's *This is a Room* for DTF 2017.

Veronica recently directed Noelle Brown's *In Plain Sight*, an exploration of Ireland's history of mother and baby homes through the lens of architecture. She is currently working on a piece exploring the legacy of Article 41 of the Irish Constitution in collaboration with composer, Sinéad Diskin and actor/dancer, Sibéal Davitt.

Veronica is the author of *Clown Through Mask – The Pioneering Work of Richard Pochinko As Practised By Sue Morrison*, written in collaboration with Sue Morrison and published by Intellect Press, currently being translated into Spanish. She has been awarded the Prix Europa/Radio France, World Gold Medal Status New York, and a Writers' Guild of Ireland Zebbie Award for her work in radio drama.

Emmet Kirwan is an award-winning actor and playwright from Tallaght in Dublin.

He studied at the Samuel Beckett Centre, Trinity College Dublin. He first worked with Fishamble: The New Play Company twenty years ago on their play *Monged* and has worked with the company many times since and is delighted to be joining the company again for *The Leap*.

He has worked in Irish and English theatre performing many times on stages such as The Abbey, The Gate, Project, Donmar Warehouse, the National Theatre and the Soho Theatre, as well as working with leading theatre companies such as Rough Magic, Fishamble, ThisIsPopBaby, Guna Nua, Pan Pan and Barabbas.

He has numerous film and television credits most recently the films *Magpie* and *Spilt Milk*. As actor-playwright his play *Dublin Oldschool* won the Stewart Parker Trust Major Award, it toured internationally and transferred to the National Theatre in Britain. He also wrote and starred in the film version of the same name for Warrior and Element Pictures.

His most recent work as an actor and playwright *Accents* (a collaboration with the musical artist Talos) toured nationwide. His plays are published by Methuen Drama. He is also known for writing and starring in the RTÉ 2 comedy series *Sarah and Steve* for Accomplice TV.

Penny Morris is a Dublin-based actor and recent graduate of The Lir Academy, joining *The Leap* in the role of Wendy.

Recent screen credits include *The Last Disturbance of Madeline Hynde* (Nuncle Films) and *Silent Witness 28* (BBC) as Ms. Brady.

On stage, Penny was most recently seen as Joe in *Just Being Open With You* by Conor Kelly at Smock Alley Theatre.

Other recent theatre credits include Joe in *I Had a Dream I Shot You in the Head, but the Calibre Wasn't Very Big* by Conor Kelly at Smock Alley Theatre and Jessica in Geoff O'Keefe's *The Merchant of Venice* at the Mill Theatre.

Shauna Harris is a multidisciplinary artist, actor and writer. Her theatre credits include *The Giggler Treatment* (The Ark); *Passports* (Dublin Fringe/Project Arts Centre);, *Hive City Legacy: Dublin Chapter* (Dublin Fringe/Hot Brown Honey) – winner of the Dublin Fringe Festival Judges' Choice Award;and *Monsters* (Dublin Fringe/The Lir Academy), which she also co-wrote.

Shauna was a mentee on the 2024 Screen Ireland x Writers' Guild of Ireland Black Irish Screenwriters Mentorship and a 2023–24 Dublin Fringe Festival WEFT Studio artist. She was also a collaborative recipient of the 2023 Romilly Walton Masters Award and a residency from Centre Culturel Irlandais Paris in partnership with Dublin Fringe Festival.

Currently she is a mentee on the artist in the community mentorship award with Create.

Her screen credits include *Trasna na Líne* (Virgin Media/ Reblis Films); *Breeders* (Fantastic Films) and *500 Miles* (Origin Pictures).

Mary-Lou McCarthy is an actor and theatre-maker who has worked extensively across stage and screen, with a focus on new writing, physical theatre, and work for young audiences.

Stage credits include *Me, Mollser* (Abbey Theatre – national and US tour); *The Heiress* (Gate Theatre); *The Blue Boy* (Brokentalkers – Dublin Theatre Festival and international tour); *Factory Girls*, *Lovers/Winners* (The Everyman); *BigKidLittleKid*, *Still Here* (Anna Newell/Civic Theatre); *Bees! A Musical* (Willfredd/The Ark); *Record* (Dublin Theatre Festival) and *Gach Áit Eile* (Abbey Theatre). She also performed in *Bodies in Urban Spaces* (Cie. Willi Dorner, Dublin Dance Festival).

On screen, Mary-Lou played the recurring role of Úna in the IFTA-winning series *An Klondike* (TG4/Netflix – international title *Dominion Creek*) and appeared in *Wolf* (Focus Features); *Pursuit* (dir. Paul Mercier); *Fair City* (RTÉ);

The Mario Rosenstock Show (RTÉ); *Corp + Anam* and *Aifric* (TG4). She played the lead role in *Penny*, which won Best Drama at the Fastnet Film Festival.

As a writer, she was commissioned by the Civic Theatre's Ready, Steady, Show! initiative to develop her play *The Dead Letter Office*, exploring migration and belonging for ages 9+ which premiered in October 2022 and toured nationally in 2024.

Mary-Lou was artist in residence at the Centre Culturel Irlandais in Paris supported by Draíocht, and was a 2022 recipient of an Arts Council Next Generation Award.

Mary-Lou is a creative associate with the Arts Council and facilitates drama workshops for young people in schools, youth theatres and other youth settings in both the English and Irish language. She is an associate artist with Branar Theatre Company, Galway for 2025 where she will be developing new projects for young audiences.

Deirdre Dwyer is a theatre maker based in Waterford, Ireland.

She works as a set and costume designer, a director and a writer. She is interested in making work that is accessible to all people.

Designs in 2025 include set and costume for *The Change* (Croí Glan Integrated Dance); *Hare and Tortoise* (Barnstorm Theatre); *A Day in May* (TUD).

She is an artistic director of BrokenCrow, a multidisciplinary, ensemble-led theatre company, with whom she has designed and directed shows, created her own plays and produced a series of audio dramas. She is a founder member of Shakespeare Squared, a Waterford theatre collective, for whom she co-directed *Twelfth Night*, an outdoor promenade production in Waterford's Viking Triangle in September 2023.

Her training includes an MA in Theatre Design from the RWCMD Cardiff, a degree in Drama and Theatre Studies and English from UCC and participating, as the designer, in Rough Magic SEEDS3.

She was awarded the first Pat Murray Bursary in 2009 and has been awarded an Arts Council Bursary. She has been theatre artist in residence in Mary Immaculate College, Limerick, Garter Lane Arts Centre, Waterford and Centre Culturel Irlandais, Paris.

She is the street theatre programmer for Spraoi International Arts Festival which brings artists from all over Ireland and around the world perform throughout the city of Waterford for free each August bank holiday.

She teaches design and related theories to students in UCC and has guest lectured at Mary Immaculate College Limerick, IADT and SETU and Berridge Gap Year Programme, France.

She is a founder member of the Irish Society of Performance Designers (ISPD).

Suzie Cummins is a Dublin-based lighting designer for theatre, dance and events. She has worked as a designer in Ireland for almost a decade.

Previous work with the company: *Breaking* by Amy Kidd as part of Dublin Theatre Festival 2024.

Other theatre credits include *Lovesong* (Gate Theatre); *Static* (Abbey Theatre); *The Playboy of the Western World, Super Bogger, Danty Dan, Turry Flynn, Trad* (Livin' Dred Theatre Company); *Lost Lear, The Wrens* (Dan Colley and Riverbank); *The Making of Mollie, The Race* (The Ark); *Afterwards, Absent the Wrong* (Once Off Productions); *Every Brilliant Thing* (Abbey Theatre); *After Taste* (National Youth Theatre; Abbey Theatre); *The Secrets of Primrose Square* (Pat Moylan

Productions); *Minseach* (Sibéal Davitt); *Before You Say Anything* (Malaprop); *Minefield, Charlie's a Clepto* (Clare Monnelly).

Associate lighting design credits include: *DruidO'Casey* (Druid Theatre); *Party Scene* (ThisIsPopBaby).

Denis Clohessy has previously worked with The Abbey Theatre, The Gate Theatre, Fishamble, Once Off Productions, Rough Magic, CoisCéim, Junk Ensemble, Corn Exchange, Northlight Theatre, Chicago and Beijing Children's Art Theatre. He won the Irish Times Theatre Award for Best Soundscape in 2011 and 2019 and was a nominee in 2015. Denis was an associate artist with the Abbey in 2008 and was a participant on Rough Magic's ADVANCE programme in 2012.

Composition for film and television includes the feature films *One Night in Millstreet*, Fastnet Films; *Older than Ireland*, Snack Box Films; *His and Hers*, Venom Film; *The Irish Pub*, Atom Films; and the animation series *Will Sliney's Storytellers*, Fastnet Films.

Jim Culleton is the artistic director of Fishamble, for which he has directed many productions, winning Olivier, The Stage, Scotsman Fringe First and Irish Times Best Director awards. Jim has also directed for the Abbey, the Gaiety, the Belgrade, Kennedy Center, Staatstheater Mainz, 7:84 Scotland, Audible, BBC, RTÉ, Trafalgar Theatre (West End) and IAC/Symphony Space (Broadway).

Laura MacNaughton has worked in the professional arts sector for over twenty years in theatre, film and dance. She has worked primarily as a general manager, producer and programmer. Laura has worked at a senior level in multiple arts organisations, these include The Gate Theatre, Dublin Dance Festival and the O'Reilly Theatre. Laura is a drama facilitator and director with Belvedere College Drama

Department. Most recently, she directed *Bringing Down the House* by Todd Wallinger. Laura currently sits on the Arts Council Peer Panel for Theatre and the Producers Working Group for the Performing Arts Forum. Laura is also a guest lecturer in theatre with the UCD Ad Astra Programme for exceptional students. She holds a science degree from Trinity College Dublin and is a classically trained musician and associate of Trinity College London in music performance. Laura's most significant and favourite role however is Mammy to Marianne (aged 4¾).

Laura is the producer at Fishamble: The New Play Company and previous Fishamble credits include *In Two Minds* (2023), *Taigh/Tŷ/Teach* (2024), *BREAKING* (2024) and *The Black Wolfe Tone* (2025).

Evie Mc Guinness has worked as a stage manager for theatre for the last ten years. She graduated with a distinction from The Lir Academy's Stage Management and Technical Theatre course in 2016. She has worked with The Abbey, The Gate, Landmark, Rough Magic, Pan Pan, Collapsing Horse, The Local Group, Brokentalkers, ThisIsPopBaby and Livin' Dred. Her previous work includes *Masterclass* by Brokentalkers (Dublin Fringe Festival, Edinburgh Fringe Festival, RISING Festival, Sydney Theatre Festival); *A Very Old Man With Enormous Wings* by Dan Colley (Edinburgh Fringe Festival, national tour, Imaginate, Auckland Arts Festival) and *Lost Lear* by Dan Colley (Dublin Theatre Festival, national tour, Aotearoa Festival).

Eoin Kilkenny has toured across Ireland and the world with theatre productions from Landmark Productions, Rough Magic Theatre Company, Fishamble: The New Play Company, CoisCéim Dance, Abbey Theatre and many more. He has worked at some of the best festivals at the Traverse Theatre Edinburgh during the Festival Fringe, Galway International Arts Festival, Melbourne International Arts

Festival, Dublin Fringe Festival and London International Festival of Theatre. He trained as a production manager with the Rough Magic SEEDs programme, working on their productions in Dublin, Belfast and New York. He is a product of UCD Dramsoc and has completed an MA in Producing at the Royal Central School of Speech and Drama.

Steph Ryan has worked in theatre for many years and with many companies including CoisCéim, Rough Magic, Abbey/Peacock Theatres, OTC and INO to name a few. Work with Fishamble includes *Handel's Crossing, The End of the Road, Noah and the Tower Flower, Spinning, Little Thing Big Thing, Invitation to a Journey* (a co-production with CoisCéim, Crash Ensemble and GIAF); *Mainstream, Rathmines Road, On Blueberry Hill, Embargo, Duck Duck Goose, In Two Minds, Heaven, Breaking* and Pat Kinevane's *Forgotten, Silent, Underneath, Before and King.*

Allie Whelan is the marketing, outreach and engagement manager at Fishamble: The New Play Company. Allie has worked on *Mustard, King, In Two Minds, Breaking, Outrage, Heaven, Fight Night, Not Beckett* and *The Black Wolfe Tone* with Fishamble. She has previously worked in marketing, social media and content creation roles with Dublin Fringe Festival, Poetry Ireland, Landmark Productions, Pan Pan, Glass Mask Theatre, The RDS Visual Art Awards and Music Network Ireland.

Chloe Naomi is an interdisciplinary director and theatre maker. Her work merges dramaturgical research with experimental theatricality to create relevant, playful and immersive theatre. She trained in The Lir Academy's MFA Theatre Directing programme after receiving her BA in Drama, Theatre and Performance Studies with English from the University of Galway. Chloe is the artistic director of

Ciaróg Productions which strives to produce, curate and devise new work. She has also collaborated with numerous companies across Ireland such as Druid Theatre, Active Consent, Ró Stack, Macnas and Galway International Arts Festival.

Website: https://www.chloenaomi.org/

Eva Scanlan is the executive director at Fishamble: The New Play Company.

Current and recent producing work includes *Taigh/Tŷ/Teach*, a trilingual co-production with partners in Scotland and Wales, *In Two Minds* by Joanne Ryan, *Heaven* by Eugene O'Brien, *Outrage* by Deirdre Kinahan, *The Treaty* by Colin Murphy, *Embargo* by Deirdre Kinahan, *The Alternative* by Michael Patrick and Oisín Kearney, *On Blueberry Hill* by Sebastian Barry, Fishamble's award-winning plays by Pat Kinevane *King, Before, Silent, Underneath* and *Forgotten*, and many other productions on tour in Ireland and around the world.

Eva produces *The 24 Hour Plays: Dublin* at the Abbey Theatre in Ireland (2012–present), in association with the 24 Hour Play Company, New York as a fundraiser for Dublin Youth Theatre. She has worked on *The 24 Hour Plays* on Broadway and *The 24 Hour Musicals* at the Gramercy Theatre in New York.

The Leap

Dedicated to Juno Kostick

A Note on Music

It feels like there should be musical motifs with the characters through the story to help identify key characters as they arrive or perhaps are about to arrive.

A Note on the Text

When **Wendy** *and* **Dad** *speak in italics they are sharing their thoughts with us.*

Wendy

Wendy *is in mid-air.*

'For victory!' I cried as I threw myself off the piano.

'For victory!' I cried as I threw myself through the air.

'For victory!' I cried as I threw myself
through the air from off the piano.

'For victory!' I cried as I threw myself through the air from off the piano towards the glass coffee table. I cried 'For victory!' but really spite was in my heart.

I think there was also sadness in my heart.

I should not have been on the piano. It was a digital piano,
and too much fuss had been made over it.

I had been told not to climb on the piano as it was not too safe. Sure the sides were only cardboard or something.

But the urge to throw myself from off the piano and through the coffee table was too strong. The spite and sadness in my heart were too strong.

If I did not climb on the piano, I would not be able to get a good jump at the glass coffee table and have a good chance of smashing it all to pieces.

In the air I heard my own words, 'for victory' in my ears and
I knew that I had a very good chance I would land in the
coffee table and smash it all to pieces.

It was only when I was in the air really,
    that I began to think about it.

In the air I could already feel that maybe this was not a great idea. My mother really loves that coffee table.

On the glass table I had set up all my
My Little Ponies. There are seven of them.

They are Applejack, Rainbow Dash, Fluttershy, Trixie, Princess Luna, Pinkie Pie and Twilight Sparkle.

I had loved them when I was very little. I still
loved them but felt I was too old for them and
that made me cross with them.

Perhaps it was because I was cross with them for making me love them and now I felt a bit too old for that, that I had put them out on the glass coffee table. The glass coffee table that I knew, even when I was in the air, that I was going to smash all to pieces. But maybe it was just that I had a bad heart and I thought that if I smashed everything including the coffee table, the ponies and myself then the pain would go away.

In mid-air I moved my head because
I couldn't look at the faces of the ponies.

I saw the river and the sky through the open window, and I smelt the wetness of the river as I was still in the air.

In the reflection of the slant of the open
    glass I could still see the table.

In the reflection it looked to me as if Twilight
Sparkle's wing was a hawk in the sky outside.

In the reflection of the glass it looked to me as if Applejack's tail was the tail of a fox on the bank.

In the reflection of the window it looked to me as if the copper curls of Pinkie Pie were a salmon leaping in the river.

I tried not to see them and I turned my head more.

In the little car park, I could see my dad's van.
It is a big purple van. I was sure it had not been
there just moments before.

In the air I realised that I had heard the
front door, but not really heard it somehow.

In the air I realised that I had heard footsteps coming into the little hall but that had not gone into my brain somehow.

It was only as I was in mid-air that I realised that my dad must have parked the van, let himself into the building, come up the lift, come through the door of the flat, walked down the little hall, opened the sitting room door and now he was stood there, watching me, with his mouth open as I hurled myself from off the piano, through the air.

We are a little bit back in time.

Dad *is driving.*

Dad   Now for the steep hill. I know you young people don't
be driving as yet: but to push up a hill what it is is, what you
do is, drop down a gear – down another gear – catch her on
the clutch, which is with your feet. And then if you have it
right, there's the pull of the old Ford as it makes its way up.

There's a old, surviving whitethorn tree on the right which I
use as a guide – there she is – and we're into the narrow lane
where you have to be careful in case you meet a car coming
the other way. This is all all up by the Tolka, not far from
Finglas – but you'd feel right in the country all the same.
Parp! Parp! – I'm a cautious driver and I blow the horn to let
people know I'm coming round the bend. And I've promised
my wife, Sheila is her name, to take care coming home the
last bit. You can lose concentration at the end of a long drive.
It's important to keep your concentration.

Sheila gave me these driving gloves last Christmas. I keep
them on me when driving so as to remind me of being safe
for her sake.

Okay, another right now and that's us on the old bridge. It's
a tricky one as it's a hard right angle to go on (*Demonstrates*.)
like that – and a right angle the other way to come off. Sheila
asks that I'm home before dusk is in the branches so as I can
see what I'm about.

'Good afternoon, Mr Fox.' – Mr Fox is out and about.

Now the last long lane-way under the hedges before the
sudden clearing and finally – here we are – the new build
apartments, up the Tolka. It's a beautiful spot really, but the
apartments aren't everyone's choice.

That's me parked and I'm trying to shake that I feel bad that
I had been away for such a long day during the holidays. I
hope Wendy hasn't upset the place too much what with

Sheila and myself having to be out to work. It's tough on her to be in the flat alone but I tell myself she's twelve now.

'Good afternoon, Missus Hawk.' – The old hawk is out and about.

The apartment hadn't been part of the life-plan at all at this stage. It's right on an old special spot on the Tolka where there's a willow I used to climb, and a weir beyond. Dublin was far more country 'til the week before last. 'Til very recent in any case.

See, I'd been busy making and fitting new glass displays, for them sweet shops with all the candies and such. Good quality trim, brass and hardwoods. All proper. I knew when they had to put a sign to stop the children standing up and putting their hands on the glass that we had a mighty hit. So it seemed like we were going up in the world and the apartment was sold to us as a step on the ladder, like.

Anyways, a weir is like a human-made waterfall that was made in olden times to drive the water towards a mill. They're done in such a way as to allow salmon to leap back up them so they can find their way to the spawning grounds from time to time.

But still, I'd only a small outfit, and the multinationals came in with the their laser cutting and MDF and we can't compete really, I've had to go back to driving around – like now – with samples in the back and going further and further to smaller and smaller places, and looking for business. So we ended where we are and Wendy still in the little rom, which was meant for when she was a babby.

The piano would be a good example. We wanted one for Wendy as she grew up as we had those kind of notions, ya know, but when it came to it we had to settle for what we could. Wendy took a turn against it anyway.

I feel bad because me and Sheila have to work all the days which leaves Wendy alone a lot.

(*He takes the gloves off and kisses them.*) That's for luck. Now, where's me keys.

'What is it, Mrs Salmon? I thought you were beyond those old leaps.'

Hawk in the sky, fox on the bank, salmon on the weir.

There's something out of shape, isn't there?

Cummon! Key in the door, cumon, won't be too bad, wait on the lift, race down the hall. Soon be alright, in we go, nice cup of tea. Almost relieved already at worrying for nothing and . . . open the door.

And there's Wendy flying through the air and she lands in the glass and shatters the world all to pieces.

Wendy   'I didn't mean to do it!'

I sat amongst the smashed glass and the ponies were scattered all over. Now you'd think that having been caught in the act of going through the table, I was ripe for a bad telling off, and there was nothing more to be said. But the strangest feeling came over me that whatever I was, I was not sorry I had done it. And what I certainly didn't want to get into was the feelings that were in my heart and all that. They really weren't anyone else's business. And, now I thought about it, if they were my father and mother's business they should have listened more when I said I didn't want to go to a school that was miles away, with a bag no one could lift in a place where my friends couldn't visit because Mam and Dad were out all the time and they didn't really trust me, and stuck in a room where I was trapped in a baby's life.

So there's me with hot and cold feelings running all through me and I think the best thing is to close all that off. I had done it and it was too complicated to explain to Dad, so I thought the best thing was to say whatever was needed to get away with it. And with any luck it would all go away.

It was like my heart had exploded and monsters had come out and so I just shoved everything back in and closed the door.

Change in their stage relationship. They are both 'there' now.

Dad   So I looks at the pieces all in front of me and thought well now that's a lot of splinters. That's a lot to put back together.

Wendy   I burst into tears. Dad came over. I knew he was trying to look me in the eyes, but I didn't want to be looked in the eyes, not then. I wouldn't have minded a hug though. Anyway, his shape was in front of me and he said

Dad   What happened, Wendy? And she said,

Wendy   It was an accident.

Silence.

Wendy   And he said, and to be fair to him he wasn't roaring or anything,

Dad   Try again, Wendy, what happened? And I tried not to think about the damage.

Wendy   It was an accident. And it wasn't so much I was lying as I just wanted the conversation to be over. And he said

Dad   Once more, Wendy chuck, what happened?

Wendy   I had an accident. And what with him obviously not believing me a bit of me closed off. And, maybe if he'd started off with a hug I might have blurted it all out but he hadn't. So there I was, angry with him in spite of all. And I thought, well it's best if we just believe it was an accident – or at the very least I didn't mean it – and then there's no need to talk about it ever again and what's so very wrong with that?

I felt the little cut where one piece of glass had gone in. It stung.

Dad   Now I'm not the worst with words. I don't mind the old chat. But I tell you, I didn't know what to say then. Once she'd stuck to the story that it was an accident I felt it was going to be very difficult to unstick it. I mean, once I'd said I didn't think that was true, she'd just say it was and then where would we be?

So I thought about how to set about fixing things and what a very long journey that was going to be and what a long way we'd be going and I thought best concentrate on that. Delicate situation and all not to drive her further away anyway.

'Would you mind standing up?'

Wendy   Okay.

Dad   Would you mind standing still for a little bit?

Wendy   Okay.

Dad   Just wait.

Dad *goes off and comes back with a rucksack, old newspapers, dustpan and brush and a pair of tweezers.*

Okay, let's have a look at you.

He looks her over.

No harm done?

Wendy   No.

Dad   No cuts at all?

Wendy   No.

Dad   *I'd liked to have stopped there, but I couldn't not ask.* Wendy, when . . . I wonder . . . you didn't catch the glimpse of a hawk at all?

Wendy   *What's that got to do with anything?* No.

Dad   And did you catch a glimpse of a fox at all?

Wendy   *How does he know?* No.

Dad   And, last one, a salmon jumping out of the water by any chance?

Wendy   *This is weird.* No. No stupid animals.

Dad   *And with each answer she goes slipping further away and it's looking so much harder to get her back. Well, well.* Let's see, big pieces first.

Dad *pads the rucksack with paper and starts to put big pieces of glass in.*

Dad   Here, you have the tweezers and get the very little bits.

Dad *busies himself with the dustpan and brush. A bit to her surprise* **Wendy** *is helping.*

Wendy   Dad, why can't we just hoover it up?

Dad   I suppose we need all the bits to fix it.

Wendy   Is it going to be fixed?

Dad   Well, do you want it fixed?

Wendy   . . .

Dad   . . .?

Wendy   I don't know.

Dad   Okay. Now give me a hand with the frame. Carefully.

They set up the frame of the coffee table so it is like a little door.

Dad   Right – Wendy, have you made chicken nuggets?

Wendy   I'm allowed use the cooker!

Dad   Right. They may come in handy.

Wendy   For snacks?

Dad   For later. Put three in the rucksack. Please. Two bananas would be good.

She puts three chicken nuggets in the rucksack. He puts in two bananas.

Dad   And (*He doesn't like this.*) do we have a needle at all?

Wendy   In the sewing basket.

Dad   Right. And a bit of cloth with that.

Now, lookit, come round here. No, not through.

Wendy   Dad?

Dad *is shifting the frame of the coffee table so it frames light.*

Have a bit of fun with this. **Dad** *with help from* **Wendy** *frames the door around a space that opens up. For example, a patch of light might be framed from the sun shining through a window and the coffee table fame is placed the other way up on the floor and, when exactly filled with light, forms a pathway through the world.*

When **Dad** *goes through frame he makes sure the rucksack does not touch either side.*

Dad   Yes?

Wendy   Is that a door?

Dad   It is.

Wendy   Has it always been a door?

Dad   It has. We just have to get it shifted it to the right place.

That's it.

They come out by an oak tree, with a willow tree just beyond on the river bank. It is this world but more colour saturated, more vigorous and yet louring.

Dad   Right, will you pull us some acorns?

Wendy   I can't reach them.

Dad   I'll lift you. Here.

Wendy   You get them.

Dad   Can't touch 'em, has to be your hands.

Wendy   If you say so.

Lifted by **Dad**, **Wendy** *gets three acorns. Quick note: through to the end of the adventure,* **Dad** *grows younger and more vigorous.*

Dad   Me back.

Dad *turns to the willow over the river.*

Dad   Okay, let's see if it's still there at all – now we need to climb along that branch. You go first.

Wendy   I'm not sure I can.

Dad   Look, Wendy. I don't mind if there's things you can't say now, can't tell me – I mean I do mind but I understand – but don't pretend you've never climbed this tree. For one thing I've seen you.

Wendy   Okay.

They climb – **Dad** *is struggling a bit as he has lost the knack.*

Dad   Now, get the acorns and drop one on the water.

Wendy   Okay.

She drops one. Nothing.

Dad   Another.

Drops another. Nothing. But what is that bubble in the water?

Dad   Last one, just a bit further out.

Last one. A mouth takes it. The salmon appears. It is large, old and gold.

Dad   Now ask it d'way across the river.

Wendy   Sorry?

Dad   Ask the salmon d'way across the river. Politely. With manners.

Wendy   Really?! Show us the way across the river please, Mr Salmon.

Dad   In salmon! In salmon! It doesn't speak human. And it's Nana Salmon.

Wendy   In . . . but . . . we haven't done salmon at school.

Dad   Okay, ur, hmm. Pop, pop, pwarp, pop, pup.

Salmon   Pop, pwarp, pup-pup, pop.

Wendy   It spoke!

Dad   Pop, pwarp, wharp, pop.

Wendy   What is it saying?

Dad   You need to ask the way.

Wendy   Why?

Dad   It's not my adventure. It's your adventure.

Wendy   Are we on an adventure?

Dad   We are. And you need to be doing the asking. Repeat after me. Pop.

Wendy   Pop.

Dad   Pwarp.

Wendy   Pwap.

Dad   No, Pwarp. Otherwise you're telling her want the toilet.

Wendy   Pwarp.

Dad   Wharp, pop-pup? *(Pause.)* Wharp, pop-pup?

Wendy   Wharp, pop-pup?

Salmon   Pop, pop – whaar, whaar, whaar.

Dad   Okay, great. Now step carefully in every spot just under where the salmon leaps.

Wendy You mean in the river?

Dad Yes.

Wendy Like on stepping stones?

Dad Yes, I suppose like on stepping stones.

Wendy But I can't see them. Am I supposed to see them?

Dad No, that's why we need help from Nana Salmon. There are paths in this world we can't find without help.

Wendy Dad.

Dad Yes.

Wendy But I can't.

Dad I'll do the first couple if it helps. Look.

Salmon *leaps.* **Dad** *steps onto the water. Reaches up to help.* **Wendy** *steps down. They hop, as if on the stepping stones, following the* **Salmon** *as it leaps upstream and across the river.*

Wendy *Dad hops from spot to spot and I follow. There's something different about him. Most of the time at home he's just tired. Now there's, a bit of bounce to him. He looks strange. Maybe it's just because I'm looking at him properly – who really looks at their dad anyway? Why would you?*

Dad *I watch my old guide the salmon as she makes her way up the river and I am filled with a great sadness and strong comfort. It's good to have friends. But she is old now and I can see that the leaps are taking it out of her, it's a struggle for her with the current. I could say something, but I think she wouldn't take kindly to that. Anyway, it's afternoon now and if the night comes with everything broken I don't like to think about the world falling apart at all.*

They have crossed.

Dad Okay. Pop, pwap, pup.

Salmon Pop, pwarp, pwupp.

Dad   Really? That's very good of you. She says you can take a scale.

Wendy   One of her scales.

Dad   Yes, you pick one.

Wendy   Will it hurt?

Dad   I don't think she'll mind.

Wendy   Okay.

She picks a scale from the **Salmon***.*

Dad   Well, put it in your mouth.

Wendy   Okay.

Wendy *puts the scale in her mouth.*

Salmon   She's a fine girl.

Dad   We think so.

Wendy   I can understand you!

Dad   Yes, well, it's important to speak salmon. It's not really one language though, it's more a language cluster with local variations. You'll have to practise to keep it up.

Wendy   Dad?

Dad   Yes?

Wendy   Will you stop explaining things.

Dad   Sorry, habit. Okay, on we go.

Thanks, old friend. Much appreciated. Goodbye.

Salmon   Perp!

Dad   *I only wish Wendy had thought to thank the salmon too, but she's wrapped up in herself still so I suppose it can't be helped. And I see that my golden friend is tired now and can only float back down and has turned a little on her side which looks wrong for her.*

And maybe it's just as well Wendy is looking ahead of her and not back. Yes, maybe just as well.

Wendy   *I've never been on this part of the bank. I don't suppose there's any way to get here. It's a lot more tangled that it looks from the other side. I think at night it would be scary. It's getting a bit dark now. I wish Dad would just stop staring back down the river.*

Dad *holds a pouch of the rucksack open.*

Dad   Now, take the nuggets and lay them out.

Wendy *takes the nuggets and lays them out, glancing at* **Dad** *who notes. There's a disturbance in the woods. As they look one way the* **Fox** *takes a nugget. It is gone. And again. And a third time.* **Dad** *is going increasingly worried.*

Fox   Rap, rap, rap-riff rap.

Wendy   Dad!

Dad   Yes?

Wendy   What's that?!

Fox   Rouff, rowff.

Dad   That's Mr Fox. Well, Monsieur Fox. All foxes are French. From France – it's complicated. Hang on. Rouff, roouw, riouu.

Fox   Rip, rup. Rip.

Wendy   Dad, how is it you've never said you can speak fox?

Dad   Well, I do it so rarely. And not nearly so well as your mother.

Wendy   Mam can speak fox?

Dad   Your mother has many skills. But we need to get on – Row, riff, grrrick.

Fox   Rougher, rouw.

Dad   Very good. Now you need to ask the way.

Wendy   Dad?

Dad   Yes.

Wendy   What happens if I don't ask?

Dad   Well, I suppose we're stuck here.

Wendy   And then what would happen?

Dad   I don't know, Wendy. I think we'd be stuck and I don't know any other way out.

Wendy   Unless I ask?

Dad   Yes, that is in your power.

Wendy   . . .

Dad *smiles.*

Wendy   Okay.

Dad   Right, repeat after me. Urrip.

Wendy   Urrip.

Dad   Rouff.

Wendy   Rouff.

Dad   Row (*Rhymes with 'ow' as in 'now'.*), row, grrrr.

Wendy   Row, row, garrr.

Dad   No, that's, you're asking if you can leave the table. Row, row, grrrr.

Wendy   Row, row, grrrr.

Fox   Grrr-urruurr.

Dad   Now hang on to his tail and I'll hold your foot.

They struggle through the undergrowth.

Wendy   *I hate this. It's dark, there's thorns. I don't know what I'm stepping on. The fox smells – smells old and wet and carpety. That's*

*it like a mouldy old carpet. This is, this is. Gloomy. I don't like it,
but the fox is dragging me and I'm dragging Dad. And what's this
about anyway? All this to fix the table. I'm not sorry I smashed it.
Not sorry at all. So why am I getting my knees all grazed for
anyway? I mean, jumping across the river wasn't so bad, but this is
just, just, wretched.*

Dad   *I was remembering the first time I came this way. I hated it.
Haa-aa-ted it. I was a lot younger then and so was M. Fox. He's
got old.*

Fox   Ummrouff, raw, raw, row.

Dad   Thank goodness.

Wendy   Are we there?

Dad   Well, we're through the bushes.

Wendy   Do I have thorns in my hair?

Dad   Let's see – a bit, yeh.

Fox   Brough, bri, bri.

Dad   Really? That's very kind of you. He says you can have
a hair from his tail.

Fox   Grough.

Wendy   Will I have to eat it?

Dad   No, that would be stoopid. You tie it around your little
finger.

Wendy   Okay.

She does so.

Fox   She's a fierce little mademoiselle, isn't she?

Dad   Headstrong, yes.

Wendy   Are you talking about me?

Dad   Sorry. Habit.

Fox   Bon voyage, ma petite.

Wendy   He is French.

Dad   Yes, well, of French heritage, the foxes came over with the Normans, you see. We know from manuscripts that the first fox was Reynard. His great, great and so on, grandfather.

Wendy   Dad.

Dad   Yes?

Wendy   Stop educating me.

Dad   Never.

Wendy   *There's a funny little cliff and the top of it bends away so I can't see how high it is at all.*

Now what?

Dad   We wait to just before sunset.

Wendy   *And he sits down and faces the setting sun. And again he looks less and less like Dad and more like, more like. A goblin or something. He's more earthed, that's what he is. Like a piece of stone has been carved and his hair is moss and his eyes are like a dark pool. I've no idea who my dad is at all.*

Anyway, we're at the base of the cliff now and I can't see how we're going to climb it and the fox is gone so there's no going back. I'm actually quite proud of my manners and I don't like to be rude but – pheerrr-eeuuuw – I'm glad that smell is gone.

Dad   *I watch my old friend go and his red coat now is nearly all smeared with grey. He doesn't walk too well either. There's a hitch in his hips. Well, well, it's a last hurrah for all of us, maybe.*

And though we're doing well, I do wish Wendy had said thank you to M. Fox. There's a power in that.

In my heart I feel for Wendy. Where she's at, like. I'm sorry to say that the answer to that is still very, very far away. And I can feel the wound she doesn't want to talk about.

Dad *takes out the bananas.*

Wendy   Who eats the bananas?

Dad   We do.

Wendy   Dad?

Dad   Yes?

Wendy   Why are we waiting for sunset at all?

Dad   Well, we have to see two sisters.

Once there were these two sisters. Day and Night. And they ha-aa-ted each other. Always fighting. It was terrible. And when Night was winning, the world was dark. And when Day was winning, the world was all light and nobody knew where they were.

And this world and the otherworld were all mixed up too and nobody knew their proper place either. It was a shockin mess and lives were terrible.

Down the line, by the way, is also the story of how your mother and I met and how I saved a salmon, a fox and a hawk from this and that, and in the end how you were born.

But, going back, the short of it is that in the end there was a big council and it was agreed that the two of them each had to give way to the other and so dawn and twighlight were invented. Night gives way to Day and Day gives way to Night.

And those are the hinges of the world and that is the time also when the otherworld touches this world and this world touches the otherworld. Just as it gets light and just as it gets dark.

And to seal the deal, between them they created glass. They made a mighty necklace originally.

Then with this and that and down through the ages it became other things, and your mother's table at last.

That table is the point where the two worlds touch – you can see one reflected in the other. It links them, but it keeps them apart. In order.

Wendy   And I've broken it.

Dad   You've broken it.

Wendy   What will happen if it stays broken?

Dad   I don't know. Chaos, I imagine. Without you, Wendy, our [*his and his wife's*] world will be chaos.

Wendy   Dad.

Dad   Yes?

Wendy   I'm still not really sorry I broke it.

Dad   I know.

Wendy   Why don't you listen to me?

Dad   We listen . . .

Wendy   You don't hear.

Dad   Fair.

Wendy   But I am sorry if you're upset.

Dad   That's very kind of you. What should we have listened to?

Wendy   Don't know. Unhappiness. All the same, it was never really about you or Mam neither. Sorry.

Dad   I did wonder. I did wonder what we'd done wrong.

Wendy   Oh nothing. Nothing. Apart from the listening. You're great . . . it's just I don't want to talk about it.

Dad   That's okay. I'm not trying to fix things. I'm just trying to bring us to a place where things can be fixed.

Wendy   And what happens if I don't want to go on?

Dad   Then we stay here.

Wendy   Okay. Tell me what's up there on the cliff.

Dad   At the top of the cliff is a cave.

Wendy   Okay. And what is in the cave?

Dad   Not what. Who.

Wendy   Who are we going to see in the cave?

Dad *looks* **Wendy** *in the eyes and gives it both barrels.*

Dad   Gods, Wendy. We're going to see gods. Er, Wendy. Now you have to prick your finger with the needle and put blood on the cloth.

Wendy   Really?

Dad   This one needs blood.

Wendy   My blood is it, Dad?

Dad *nods.*

Dad   You could use your cut.

Wendy   You don't know about that.

Dad   Then use the needle.

Wendy *does it.*

A great **Hawk** *comes.*

Hawk   Kreeee-eeeeirreeeee-eeee-aaaeeeeee-eeeee.

KREEEEEE-AAAAEEEEEEEEE-
AAAAAAAEEEEEEEE-
ERIEEEEAAAAYYYYYY

KREEEEEE-
AAAAEEEEEEEEE-
AAAAAAAEEEEEEEE-
ERIEEEEAAAAYYYYY

Dad   Good to see you too.

Wendy   She is the most beautiful thing I have ever seen.

Dad   Eee-eeeria-ayyyeeee.

Wendy   Right. So you speak hawk. Obvs.

Dad   It's a life skill.

Hawk   Eeek-eyiriay-eee-eeeria-cl-cl-cl.

Dad   Okay, repeat after me.

Wendy   If I want to.

Dad   Well, yes.

Wendy   . . . Dad.

Dad   Yes?

Wendy   Are there really gods?

Dad   Oh yes, of course, of course, there really are gods.
You'll see me scared.

Wendy   Okay.

Dad   Eee-ayya-cl-eeee.

Wendy   Eee-ayya-cl-eeee.

Dad   Kree-ayy-ah.

Wendy   Kree-ayy-uh.

Dad   Close, but you're asking if you can go to bed.
Kree-ayy-ah.

Wendy   Kree-ayy-ah.

Dad   Now we both hold on to her tail.

Dad *and* **Wendy** *hold on to the tail of the* **Hawk** *and they fly.*

Wendy   *Dad said he would be scared. I don't think he ever said
that before. I'm scared all the time. For the first time maybe, I think,
maybe I'd like to let that go. This flying bit is good. Really good. I
can see for miles and miles and I can feel the wind rush right*

*through me. Cold and kind of blasting. So for a bit I let go. I don't
mean of the tail – that would be a disaster. No, I mean for a bit I
can let go of the fear.*

Dad   *Wendy has closed her eyes. She looks beautiful. She said my
good friend the hawk was beautiful but she's not so beautiful to me
as her. I love no one so absolutely as her . . . well, well. Let's see
what can be done.*

Wendy   *All too soon we're at the mouth of the cave. It's very dark
in there. But there's a glow also.*

Hawk   Eee-kreee-kriiiick.

Dad   Really, that's very kind of you. She says you may take a
feather.

Wendy   Will I be able to speak hawk?

Dad   Yes, and fly in special circumstances. Tie it into your
hair.

Wendy *ties the feather into her hair.*

Dad   I say flight, but really it's the ability to find certain
paths through the sky. It's all based on the world tree . . .

Wendy   Dad.

Dad   Yes?

Wendy   Stop explaining things.

Dad   Sorry.

Wendy   The magic is enough.

Dad   Oh.

Hawk   Tá sí fásaithe uait. [She's outgrown you.]

Dad   Had to happen.

Hawk   Ní chasfaimid le chéile arís. [We won't meet again.]

Dad   I expect not. Tá a fhios agat go bhfuil mo bheannacht
ar m'iníon. [My blessing is on my daughter, you know.]

Hawk   Tuigim. [I understand.]

Dad   *And she's gone. With a long lazy spiral down through the air and even you, old friend and a far greater power than me, even you – the strength is going from your wings. And I do wish Wendy had thought to say thank you but she's facing into the cave now and maybe facing forward is just as well for her. Plenty of time to look back when all is done.*

Wendy   *The problem with adults is that they talk about you as if you can't hear them. I wish they wouldn't. I look at Dad.*

Pass me the rucksack.

Dad   Okay.

Wendy   *It's heavy. And we step into the cave.*

Wendy *and* **Dad** *move into the cave. We meet the twin gods of* **Day** *and* **Night**.

As the day is ending, **Day** *is still slightly dominant but by the end* **Night** *is dominant. They hate each other but can't live without each other. Hate isn't really the right word. Would fly after each other if they weren't so tightly bound to each other.*

Day   Well. Well, well well.

Night   You're back.

Dad   I am.

Day   You never visit us.

Night   Unless you want something.

Dad   Don't I?

Day   How's your wife?

Dad   Very well.

Night   Liar.

Day   Cup of tea?

Dad   No thanks.

Night   Won't even take a cup of tea.

Day   Tea of the gods not good enough for him.

Night   He has notions.

Wendy   *I have to say, my dad is actually talking to gods and doing a pretty good job of it. Go Dad. He looks like, he looks like, he looks like a proper man, that's what he looks like.*

Dad   The glass is broken.

Night   Broken how?

Silence.

Day   Who broke it?

Silence.

Dad *gestures for* **Wendy** *to step forward. She takes out the rucksack and tips out all the glass.* **Night** *and* **Day** *stare at it.*

Night   Why didn't you bring all of it.

Day   There's a piece missing.

Dad   It's all in this cave.

Night *and* **Day**   Oh.

They register **Wendy**.

Dad   Can you fix it?

Day *and* **Night**   Of course. But it won't be the same.

Day *and* **Night** *fix the glass. What this looks like is the glass melting and then spinning in streams like candy floss being woven when it's hot, the colours of sunset as twighlight is woven into it and as it cools it becomes glass again but a different shape than at the start.* **Day** *and* **Night** *look like weavers.*

It comes back as a smokey vase.

There is a chip in the glass.

Day   Quick now. The last piece.

Night   Last piece please, Wendy. Where is it?

Day   If you leave it, it will be pure Night, and she'll be in charge. A dark world.

Night (*a temptation*)   Welcome to the void.

Day   Oh drama-rama. Now, Wendy. There's already a dark tinge.

Wendy   Is that so bad?

Day   For you and for everyone. A dark tinge to the world.

Night   I'm stronger, the world will be darker.

Day   Don't bring us to the abyss. (*To* **Night**.) Or it's war.

They face each other down.

Night *and* **Day**   The last piece please, Wendy.

Wendy   *And I'm about to throw myself off the piano again and I feel like what I felt like again and I'm suddenly angry and humiliated and ashamed really. And it's because my heart has opened up again and it is all flooding out and I'm not really happy with myself and I feel the sliver of glass move inside me and – oh – oh – how very close to my own heart that fragment has got and I can feel it work its way back out towards the wound and it's very painful and they're all looking at me and I hate that. And then I think that there must be something in me for the salmon to have helped, and for the fox to have helped and the beautiful hawk.*

I should have said thank you.

Dad *registers this.*

Wendy   *And the sliver is out and the glass is made.*

Night   Don't leave it so long next time.

Day   Visit us when it's not an emergency.

Night   Have a cup of tea.

Dad   I won't be back this way.

Night *and* **Day**   Why not?

Dad   My time in this world is over.

They laugh in is face.

Night *and* **Day**   Why would you ever think that?

Dad   I'm passing it on now. To her.

Night *and* **Day**   Her? Really? Are you sure?

Dad   Yes.

Wendy   I don't want you to, Dad. It's your world.

Dad   It was my world. Now it's yours. That's what I've been doing. You can speak to salmon, you can run with the fox, you can fly with the hawk. Gods will give you tea.

Wendy   What if I don't want it?

Dad   It's still yours.

Day *and* **Night**   Put it in your room. But you, Dad, we haven't finished with you – you've an old man adventure yet.

Dad   It never ends?

Day *and* **Night**   Of course not. Off you go, for now.

Dad (*to* **Wendy**)   All yours.

Wendy   But it's too much.

Dad   It was too much for me once. But I carried that load. Come on, let's go.

Wendy   For now. For today.

Dad   Okay. Let's go.

Wendy (*to* **Night** *and* **Day**)   Thank you.

Night *and* **Day**   She's very polite. Not like you.

You never said thanks.

Dad *and* **Wendy** *are on the way home.*

Dad   Well, how do you feel?

Wendy   Well now, that's a question. To be honest, there's probably too much to process to say I feel this or that about it. It's certainly been something.

Dad   Was it an accident?

Wendy   No. I did it because I was unhappy.

Dad   And when you were . . . (*indicates leaping*) . . . you saw the salmon, the fox and the hawk.

Wendy   Yes, I did see those things.

And as we go I look for them again.

I see no hawk in the sky, but I see an egg in a nest.

I see no fox in the bush, but I see a pup in the den.

I see no salmon in the stream, but I see spawn in the water.

I am a bird in the storm, I am fur amongst the thorns, I am the warrior in the cold.

They are back. A change.

Dad   Well, that's good enough for today. The vision is there, Wendy, if you ever need it. The glass is different. The world is a bit darker, you're a bit stronger. It will have to do.

Wendy   I don't know what I feel about that either.

Dad   Here, hold the vase.

Wendy *holds it.*

Dad   Would you like to smash it?

A moment.

Wendy *considers and puts it down.*

Wendy   I'm hungry.

Ends.

www.ingramcontent.com/pod-product-compliance
Lightning Source LLC
Chambersburg PA
CBHW041924090426
42741CB00020B/3473